G

And Make Disciples Of All Nations
-Matthew 28:19

GO

And Make Disciples Of All Nations
-Matthew 28:19

Dave and Gwyn Page

ARPress
ILLUMINATING IDEAS
EMPOWERING VOICES

ARPress
45 Dan Road Suite 36
Canton MA 02021
Hotline: 1(888) 821-0229
Fax: 1(508) 545-7580

Ordering Information:
Quantity Sales. Special discounts are available on quantity purchases by corporations, associations, and others. For details, contact the publisher at the address above.

Printed in the United States of America.

ISBN-13   Paperback   979-8-89330-320-9
               eBook   979-8-89330-321-6

Library of Congress Control Number: 2024900508

Table Of Contents

In Memoriam vii

Recipes from Abroad 68

Ukrainian Borsch 70

About the Authors...71

In Memoriam

This book is in memory of our son, Carey Thomas Page, who was taken from us too early. He has gone on to be with the Lord, after a critical auto accident.

It was a hot day, even for November, in this strange place. Men walked past in long robes with a strip of cloth wound round and round on their heads. I was waiting for my husband, Dave, and another missionary who had entered a building for documents. Sitting in the back seat of a car in Fes, Morocco, I waited, noticing people as they walked to and fro who looked like pictures I'd seen in my grandmother's old Bible. Men and women alike wore long robes with head coverings. It was as if I'd traveled back several thousand years to this new place. It was an eerie feeling. What was I doing here?

My husband and I volunteered to come to this North African city, when we learned there was a need for a pastor in the English-speaking church. We learned that the country was 99 percent Muslim among 30 million people and very few Christians lived here. That, in itself, was a compelling reason we should be here, working for the Lord.

We each felt the Lord leading us into missionary service before we even met. I was just seventeen years old and dedicated my life to full time mission service when my pastor preached about the lost world. He said the reason there are so many lost souls in the world is because we don't tell them the good news, either here in the States or overseas, and they were going to hell. As the church service ended, I raced up the hill to my grandparents' home, several blocks away. I was in a hurry to get there, since I didn't want my grandfather to die before I could tell him how Jesus had died for our sins. I hadn't had any soul-winning classes yet but stumbled through telling him what was in my heart. As I told him all he had to do was ask the Lord for forgiveness, he never said a word, but a big tear rolled down his cheek as I finished my pitiful presentation.

My husband felt the call as a freshman in a Baptist college and dedicated his life to mission service, even though he was a ministerial student with a part-time pastorate in southern Missouri. So, that's what we were doing here! It was also because of the verses in Matthew 28: 19–20.

> "Therefore go and make disciples of all nations, baptizing them in the name of the Father and of the Son and of the Holy Spirit, and teaching them to obey everything I have commanded you. And surely, I am with you always, to the very end of the age."

It was thirty-four years later, after college, Dave's three years in seminary, three children, twelve years of

Dave pastoring churches in four States, and twenty-two years of his years in the Navy as a chaplain.

Why did it take us so long to get to the foreign field of mission service? Because all these other things were part of God's plan too. Since we'd made a commitment to the Lord to follow Him in mission service, the Holy Spirit didn't forget.

He reminded us later on. I was reading a book called *Out of the Saltshaker and into the World* by Rebecca Pippert when the Lord spoke to me again. I could hear the Holy Spirit as He said, "When are you going to fulfill your promise of so many years ago to go to the mission field?" And, it was the second time He had spoken recently. Dave was the pastor, and we were leading a CWT (Continuing Witness Training) class. We went out after class to witness to those who did not know the Lord as their personal savior. My partner said she knew of a neighbor who needed to hear about Him, so we traveled to her home. Upon hearing scripture, read, and explained, Carla agreed to pray for forgiveness and found a new lease on life. She had been taking drugs for some time and was thrilled that Jesus could help her. At her baptism, I held a towel out to her, as she came up the baptismal steps dripping wet, and the Holy Spirit said to me, "There's more like her out there, if you'll just go find them! When will you go?"

For several weeks, I sought the Lord's guidance, wondering if my husband would think I'd lost my marbles when I'd tell him of the encounters I'd had. But what a surprise I had when he said, "Good, I've been feeling the same way! But what about your mother? We can't just throw her out in the street!"

Telling my mother about our plans would be a big shock, so I was in constant prayer about that situation. We took her into our home to live after my stepfather died, seven years prior to this. I flew to be with her before my stepdad's funeral. She came back to Virginia Beach with me after her doctor said she should go to a nursing home or home with me. She had a broken hip and ankle and was an alcoholic. But after a year or two she recovered and was sober again. She still smoked, but I figured, one out of two wasn't bad! It took her six months to get all the alcohol out of her body.

After lens implants in her eyes, she could read the newspaper without glasses and she said one day, "I feel like I died and came back to life a new person."

She divorced my father because of his drinking and beating her while in a drunken rage, every weekend for years. Mom always saw to it my brother and I were in Sunday school and church every Sunday and went with us too. But after she married my stepfather, his occasional drinking became an everyday occurrence, for both of them. He retired due to severe emphysema.

Walking down the hallway to her room, I begged the Lord to help me tell her about our calling and plans. When I informed her of the situation, she leaned forward in her recliner and said, "You've been wanting to go to the mission field since you were a teenager, *so go!*" When I asked her what she would do, she said, "There's a new retirement center being built one and a half blocks from your brother in Kansas City, so I'll go there." So, the Lord prepared her before I even informed her of the plans.

The next big hurdle was telling our two daughters. Our older daughter, Becky, was excited about our news and encouraged us. The younger one, Laura, looked a little skeptical and then said, "Well, it's better than going off to join the circus!" She encouraged us also after the initial shock wore off. If our son was still alive, he would have agreed with his sisters and encouraged us too, but he was with the Lord in heaven. He died in 1985 from injuries he received in an auto accident.

Our biggest hurdle was informing the mission board of my two craniotomies which were performed five years previously due to two ruptured mid-cerebral aneurysms. I know this is unusual to have two such surgeries and not have a disability, but I believe it was because there were two great physicians who performed the surgeries, a well-known neurosurgeon, and the Lord Jesus Christ. Dave said I did have less patience after the surgeries, and I guess he's right. (Only the right mid-cerebral artery ruptured, due to genetic weakness in the bilateral artery. An MRI showed the left side of the artery was identical with a bulge in the fork of the artery. When the neurosurgeon examined me, he said I had slurred speech, therefore he did surgery on that side first. He found the artery had not ruptured until he touched it, so it was repaired with a metal clip.) I was thankful he did the left side first, and then a week later the ruptured side. Who wants to have volunteer brain surgery later on?

We had already called the board and informed them of our calling. But since we were both in our fifties, it was dubious if they would allow us to entertain the idea. But they were eager to speak to us and invited us to a conference for those interested in going to the mission field. So after securing a "sitter" for my mother, we went to Richmond, Virginia, to the conference.

After meeting with the staff of the Foreign Mission Board, we were well on our way of starting our mission plans. We finished writing our life histories, (that we had started many years before) got medical forms filled out and looked through dozens of pleas for help in areas that needed more workers on the field. We had investigated going to Kenya, where Dave and two other pastors went on a two-week mission trip earlier. So we were looking forward to Kenya, and the director for that area agreed we could go there. We had been practicing Swahili at home after checking out the language book from the library. But at a trustees meeting, they decided we were too old to learn the language the first three years, so Dave could preach in Swahili. It was decided that we should pick another place to serve, one where Dave could preach in English. We prayed and looked over the possibilities again and chose Morocco as the place where we should serve.

Then we sent Mom on to Kansas City via air since we didn't think she could travel by car at age seventy-eight, since it was a two-day trip. She stayed with my brother and his family for a few days, until we arrived with her furniture and other things. She was all settled in and happy to be with so many people her age when we left to return to Virginia Beach.

It took longer than we imagined for our house to sell since the interest rate was high in 1991. Our mortgage payment was high, and we didn't want to have it while we were overseas.

We had many garage sales and gave furniture away to our daughters until they refused to take anymore.

Then we were off to MLC, Missionary Learning Center, just outside of Richmond, Viginia. While there, we met many wonderful couples and single women—all looking forward to going to their designated countries. We each spent a lot of time in the library, studying about the customs and beliefs of the people in those countries and listening to former missionaries speak of their experiences. After three months at MLC, we were on our way to Morocco. Our house in Virginia was sold right before we left the States.

Leaving our family members was very difficult, but the Lord saw us through it. Our youngest grandchild was only eighteen months old, and the other three were all at a sweet tender age. My parents were both in their eighties, and we were anxious about them but put them in God's hands.

When we arrived in Fes, Morocco, we were told by our sponsor that Arabic classes would begin the following week. (How about that? After we were told we were too old to learn a language!) Our sponsor's wife showed us the sights, the market, and the old city (Medina) and told us of a Moroccan woman who could cook our meals while in language school. She was to be a household cleaning woman too, staying about four hours a day. She stressed that it was a good idea to hire her while taking Arabic classes. Sounded good to me, and it was only $5 a day for her services. She came twice a week, and we were glad to have Fatima. She taught me a lot about Moroccan cooking and her homelife. When her son became gravely ill and she had to care for him, she sent her daughter, Hessna. She was in her late teens and was a marvelous cook too. Later on, she joined the English class and was teaching too.

Fes was an old city, in a valley between two mountain ranges where nearly a million people lived. The Moroccans are a friendly people, not radical, and glad for tourists and new occupants to come to their city. There are newer areas of the city as well. Nearly all the buildings and homes are constructed of concrete, whether in the old city or the new. We felt very welcome upon going there.

Views of Morocco

We lived in a furnished apartment that the mission provided, and it was efficient and comfortable. We had a large dining or living room, a good-sized kitchen and two bedrooms.

Dave took over the responsibility of preaching the first Sunday we were in the country, just two days after we arrived.

There were not many in the congregation that day, but over time it grew to around forty-five. It was only about two weeks until Thanksgiving, and I began to explore ways we could have the church members come to our apartment for the holiday. Only one other couple was from the States, but two English women said they would like to have a meal together, as well as several single women. One said they didn't celebrate Thanksgiving in England but had a Harvest Meal. So, I asked where we could get a turkey but was told no one knew of any place.

At the market, a man told me where there was a poultry house, so I went there. Not knowing the name for a turkey in Arabic, I did know how to say, *wesh andick* or "do you have?" So, I blurted out "wesh andick gobble, gobble" sounds and flapping my arms. He laughed and shook his head yes. Soon, he returned with a dressed turkey and four other men. He motioned for me to make the sound again. They all laughed, and I started to leave, looking at that poor scrawny turkey. I asked him if he had two, (and held up two fingers). He got another one, I paid him and was soon on my way with two turkeys that looked like they were about four pounds each. I later learned that the Arabic word for turkey is *be-be*.

Everyone brought food to our Thanksgiving meal, and we had a good time. There were several single people in our church, and I imagine they were thankful to have a full meal spread before them.

We started Arabic study right away. It seemed I couldn't grasp how the teacher was making the hard k sound, so we hired a tutor (a young woman who was a university student).

She was the extra help I needed to learn the language. I asked her if she had any friends who would want to come to a craft class in our apartment. She responded that she had the friends but added, "What's a craft class?" I kept thinking that if I heard the Arabic sounds, I might be able to make those hard *k* sounds too. So, I shopped for things this class needed while my tutor, Sabrina, asked her friends to come to our apartment the next Saturday. She brought eight young women, including her mother, to the class. Introductions were made, and I showed them pieces of lace, ribbons, needles, and thread I'd bought in a fabric store. We made our craft, and I enjoyed hearing their conversations in Arabic. It was good to meet them and Sabrina's mother too. She and I had a lengthy conversation with Sabrina being the translator.

Our sponsor, the man who met us at the airport, was not pleased that I had invited Moroccans to our apartment. When I asked him why, he said, "They might find out who we are." Wasn't that why we were there? I thought he might have been fearful of being kicked out of the country. But it was Dave's and my intention of working with the Moroccan people and inviting them in our home. We were not fearful since the Bible tells us "For God did not give us a spirit of timidity, but a spirit of love and self- discipline" (2 Tim 1:7).

One of the English women invited us to her apartment for a meal and said she was going to serve Yorkshire pudding. I'd read about that for years and imagined it to be something of a fruit pudding. What a surprise it was to find out it was similar to my mother's egg popovers. She served roast beef, gravy, cottage fries, and vegetables. She explained her family used to pour gravy over a slice of the Yorkshire pudding. She was from Wales and told us many interesting things about her long ministry in Morocco.

We kept taking Arabic classes and soon Christmas was drawing closer. While out walking around our apartment building one day, I found a little limb about three feet long from an evergreen tree. Picking it up, I thought it could suffice as a Christmas tree, since there were none for sale in Fes. I placed it in a glass vase and propped it up in a corner of the living room.

There were several pieces of lace and ribbon left over from the craft class, so I decorated the limb. When Sabrina came to tutor me, she asked why we had a tree in our house. I told her we Christians use the evergreen tree as a symbol of the life of Jesus Christ. He gave his life for our sins, and when we accept Him as our savior, He gives us eternal life. She had never heard that before but didn't comment since she was a Muslim.

Sabrina's mother invited us to a meal at their home and we had a delightful time. Sabrina translated for us, and we found that this family wanted the same things for their five children that we Americans want for ours—good schooling, provisions, good home life, etc. Her father was a principal at an elementary school and her mother a housewife. She fixed a delicious meal of chicken and vegetables on couscous. This meal is usually served on Fridays, the day they observe their holy day. (Recipe at end of book)

Not long after, we reciprocated and invited their family to our apartment for a meal. We served Beef Stroganoff on noodles and vegetables, and I told them it was a German meal. Sabrina's father mentioned he would like to know of an American dish, and I was stumped. The only thing I could think of was hamburgers and hot dogs. Then I explained that America is made up of people from all over the world and dishes are served from those countries.

We enjoyed many happy times getting together with Sabrina's family and our other Moroccan friends too. When we invited them for a meal it was surprising to see they had never eaten a meal on a long table with many bowls of food placed on it. They had always had a meal on a round table with one big tajine or couscous dish which everyone ate out of. So many did not know how to take a dish of carrots or meat and take a portion of it.

Our Moroccan teacher noticed his children looked in amazement at the dishes, so he just got up from his seat and reached over and put a spoon of potatoes or etc. on each plate.

Later on, we moved to a bigger apartment under the French Evangelical Church. The church building was owned by the French, and we shared the building. They're meeting early on Sunday morning, and the English church meeting later. They had a pastor who ministered to French-speaking worshippers which were mainly university students. The majority of the congregation at the English-speaking service were other missionaries from several South American countries, a family from Mexico, several American families, and tourists. With so many children coming to church, I thought it fitting that we have a Sunday School class for them, during the worship service. We didn't have much literature for the class, but I used what old books were there. One other woman offered to help teach, so we traded Sundays and taught every other week, giving us a time to attend worship service too.

The University of Fes accepted students from other French-speaking countries and offered free education. There were students from five different African countries that attended the French church service.

African students from 5 countries showing diploma

Moroccans were not allowed to come to a Christian church service, and no one was allowed by law to witness to a Moroccan. We too were not allowed to go to a Muslim Mosque.

Soon after we arrived in the country, Dave received a phone call from his brother (just seventeen months older) about his health. His prostate cancer was much worse, and the leukemia had returned. He was finally ready to talk to Dave about his spiritual welfare, so Dave told him of the plan of salvation over the phone.

Many years before, Dave tried to tell Tommy how the Lord saved him and turned his life around, but his brother didn't want to hear about it. Just to make sure Tommy understood, he called his nephew in Missouri, who called a SB Baptist pastor in Gainesville, Florida. He went to visit Tom in the hospital, prayed with him, and he finally accepted the Lord. Praise God! He died several weeks later at fifty-nine, and their older sister died of cancer about some time. We were not allowed to return to the States for their funerals because of the expense. We'd just arrived in the country several months before, so it was understandable. Dave was very close to this brother, because they had been through a lot together. So losing him was hard on Dave, but he knew Tom wasn't suffering anymore and was with his heavenly Father.

We continued our classes in Darija Arabic, the language of the common people. We studied for six months at the school in Fes and later on had a tutor come to our apartment and continue to teach us. After a while, one of the instructors wrote Bible stories for us in Arabic, and we translated them into English. He was a fine Christian man, and we thought highly of him. Many mistakes can be made with the wrong inflection or pronunciation in a word. One day, I thought I'd told our teacher I wasn't ready for class, and he said, "You aren't married?" I looked at him confused and he said, "That's what you said." Evidently the words "married" and "ready" are similar. I finally learned to say the hard k sound. The teacher told me to take a drink of water then place a pencil on my tongue. It worked, and I could eventually do it without the water and pencil! It seemed we studied Arabic the whole time we were there.

Preaching at the International Church in Fes, Morocco

Dave at work on treasurer's job

Before we moved into the apartment under the church, much remodeling had to be done. And the apartment needed a thorough cleaning. I was cleaning the bathroom floor with a scouring pad to get the grime off the terrazzo floor, when the police showed up at the door. They questioned my husband about the mission car parked outside the apartment. They hadn't seen it before so wondered where it came from. He couldn't satisfy their questioning, so they decided to take him to the police station for further questioning. Just imagine how I felt, not knowing if we would be kicked out of the country for being missionaries, or if Dave would be jailed and tortured. For several hours he was asked lots of questions and then they released him.

That whole time I kept scrubbing the floor, crying and praying the whole time that the problem would be resolved. I kept thinking of Psalm 56:3, "When I am afraid, I will trust in you." It was my birthday, and I knew many men and women would be praying for me. Our names and the country where we served were printed in a magazine called "Open Windows." This magazine is a monthly devotional guide, and I'm thankful for it and for all the faithful men and women who were praying for me on that day. We thank the Lord that He doesn't just *send* people to witness for Him, but *goes with them!*

The next year, our daughter Laura came to visit us in Morocco. She had just finished college, was about to take a job soon, and the trip was sandwiched in between. We were so happy to see her. We took her to Marrakesh, Tangier, Rabat, and south to the Sahara Desert. She was impressed with the country and the people with whom we were working. In Tangier, we visited and ate with a couple who had served in Lebanon for many years, and we had a great time. We visited several places in

Fes, too. The old medina, the old palace, harem, and grounds where the king used to live before moving to Rabat. We went to the market place, and she saw it was quite different from a supermarket in the States.

The market is an experience in itself. It's sort of like the farmer's market back home but not clean, and food is not placed in proper order as in the States. The poultry department had eggs that you count out one at a time and place in a small plastic bag. The chickens were hanging by their feet plucked but with the heads still on with flies buzzing around them. There are butchers with glass cases for the beef, mutton, and goat meat, but the French butchers have the pork cases. The only time I bought bacon was when our daughter and grandchildren visited, since it was very expensive, because it came from France. Muslims do not eat pork, so they didn't want it.

Our new apartment needed curtains, so I walked to Fes Jedid (the old city), to find fabric to make kitchen, living room, and bedroom curtains. Looking in the hanoots, (open air stores) I found the fabric section and bought some of the material I needed. But I also met many Moroccans who noticed I was from another country and commented that they knew a "little English." When I asked them if they would like to learn more, they were eager to come to class in our apartment. The arrangement was that I would teach them English, if they would help me with Arabic, no fees for either. I was anxious to help them learn English, so they might get a better job, better grade in their English class at the university, and come to know the Lord Jesus as their Savior, too. Soon, I had six students after a few months, learning English through the Laubach reading series. Frank Laubach developed this reading series so people could learn to read and eventually were able to read the Bible for themselves. Most of the students knew French but needed to know the long and short sounds of the vowels and the consonants too. They only knew the short sounds of vowels, because of the French pronunciation. When they finished the first book, they were able to read in the Book of Mark series, developed by the Home Mission Board of the SBC. It starts off saying Jesus is a teacher and introducing Him as the Son of God later in the book.

How pleased I was being able to teach these students. It reminded me of being a substitute teacher in the States and seeing the light bulb flash on when the student could read a sentence. Over time, the class grew to about ten, with the beginner class having three or four meetings on a different day.

Gwyn teaching English in Morocco

I soon realized that I was happiest when I was rubbing elbows with the nationals and before starting out the gate to walk to Fes Jedid, I prayed, "Lord, help me find someone today who needs to know you." Each time I remembered to ask Him that, He complied.

There were several groups of students coming at the same time each week and before long, there were Moroccans coming for class three days a week. There were some of the much older students I was fearful of putting in a class reading the Book of Mark, since they seemed like they might be "police plants."

Some of our students in Morocco showing diploma

Students studying the Book of Mark with Gwyn

English Students at Party

We didn't have books for the students, so I copied the day's lesson from the teacher's book on our printer. The students were pleased that they had something to take home so they could review the material. It was fourteen months before a young man named Aziz asked me after class, "Gwyn, what do you mean by saying, Take Jesus in your heart and follow Him?" He was inquiring about how to become a Christian out of earshot of other students. I was so happy, I could have danced all around the room, knowing someone finally understood! After showing him scriptures and explaining the steps of salvation, I asked him to read John 3:16, leaving out the word *whosoever* and putting his name in the verse. "For God so loved the world that He gave His one and only Son, that whosoever believes in Him shall not perish but have eternal life," (New International Version). We know that *whosoever* means every human being without exception. This was the way I came to know the Lord at the age of eleven. Then I invited him to come back that evening to speak to Dave. You see, many in that country do not believe that what a woman says is true, so I wanted Aziz to know I was speaking the truth when he heard it from my husband. That evening he returned and also a new believer, Abdul. He brought another Moroccan who wanted to know about becoming a Christian. So, two Moroccan men prayed the sinner's prayer that night, both named Aziz, who came to know the Lord as their personal Savior. Praise the Lord!

Graduation Day

A Christmas Party

Soon, two sisters came to know the Lord too. They had been faithful to come to each English class, and I considered them dear friends. They did beautiful embroidery on scarves, tablecloths, etc. I asked them if they would bring some of their handiwork and go with me to a craft store and show the owner. I told the owner several days prior to this that my friends made beautiful, embroidered items and asked if he would see them and their work. He agreed, so the girls brought their items to his store and were able to sell most everything that day. Soon they were supplying him with many beautiful things and making money for their family.

Dave had been counseling several young men who were curious about Christianity. One man came to the gate of the fence, rang the bell, and showed him a French New Testament that a tourist had given him, asking Dave to explain it to him. His name was Abdul, (whom I'd mentioned before) and he came back at the time they had agreed upon. After their discussion, Dave asked him to read several verses in the book of Matthew and to come again the next week. He returned as Dave asked and said he couldn't stop reading and read all the gospels, and half the book of Acts! He soon accepted the Lord as his Savior and entered our English class too. Dave nicknamed him Timothy.

There was a man who was Jewish and was among those to whom Dave was ministering weekly. He came to the gate quite often, asking questions about the Bible and needing more than a cup of coffee and a cookie. His father kicked him out of his house when he realized his son had accepted the Lord. Others had heard of it, whom he said were his cousins, who chased and beat him. One of them informed the police, and Raul served two weeks in jail for giving an Arabic Bible to a man who asked for it. He evangelized wherever he went.

He had no place to stay and no food. We took him in and gave him what he needed. After treating and bandaging the scrapped and bloody places on his body, he ate some supper and went to bed. The next day, he thanked us for letting him stay overnight and helping him but said he must leave due to the fact that we might get in trouble with those who beat him, and he was fearful of the police too. He came back several times and visited us but never had a permanent place to stay.

It was a pitiful situation that a father would throw his son out, and the young man had no job, place to stay, or no food. We fed him each time he came and bandaged his sores, always letting him know that we cared for him but not as much as Jesus did. Daily we prayed for his safety. He told us of a man taking him to another city where he had a house on the outskirts of town. He was treated well and given food and lodging. Then the man read to him verses from the book of Mormon. He was told that if he would join the Mormon faith, he would be given a free trip to the United States and a free college education at Brigham Young University.

Besides, they would see that he was given an opportunity of getting a business in Morocco. He said he was held captive for a few days, but eventually escaped. He didn't trust this man or believe the promises he made. He told the man he was no better off than the Muslims since they didn't believe in Jesus Christ either.

Two of our grandchildren came on their Christmas break that year. Sarah, age eleven, and Danny, eight, flew over from North Carolina. They were in awe when we took them to Fes Jedid, the old city, built around 800 AD. We explained to them that behind the stores (hanoots) the families lived in small living areas. They saw many donkeys carrying sheep skins, supplies, etc., and girls carrying bread dough on a wooden board to the forhan (ovens), so their family would have fresh bread for the next meal. I explained to them that most kitchens in a Moroccan apartment did not have ovens, so they had to use the forhan. They saw the sheep skins in the dying vats, and later on they picked out a leather jacket as their own. We took them to other parts of Morocco too, from Tangier, where they met other SB missionaries and the cities of Rabat and Marrakesh. When we went to the Sahara Desert; they marveled at the size of it. At Christmas time we had a heflah (party) to celebrate the holiday. The grandkids helped me make dozens of cookies and cakes beforehand.

At the party someone read the Christmas story, then Sarah dressed as Mary and Danny as Joseph (using our bathrobes and scarves) came into our living room. Baby Jesus was a baby doll, Sarah cuddled closely, as one of the new Moroccan believers read the Christmas story. Then we all played games and ate all those cookies, cakes and cokes.

We had lots of parties since it was a good way to invite other Moroccan friends to our get togethers. Every holiday and when they received diplomas, graduating from one level of English class to the next, we had a party. Sometimes Dave and I thought we should make up holidays, since we always had a big turnout reaching new people! Their favorite games were charades and balloon volleyball. Men sat on one side of the living room and women on the other side. The same seating arrangement happened during our Sunday afternoon worship service later on. We don't know why, it just happened.

We began to think that our apartment was like a community recreation center, where young people got together.

We were not the only Southern Baptist workers in Morocco. There was a couple in Marrakesh, two couples in Rabat, and another couple in Tangier. Our mission consisted of three churches; in Rabat, Tangier, and Fes. We were all not in the country to be missionaries, but for the men to be pastors of the international churches. It was evident at the mission meetings that there was disharmony in the mission. I overheard one woman missionary telling another that she wished the board had sent a younger couple. It's true; we did not have young children as they had, ours were grown. But we tried to do as the English did during the *Blitz*, (keep calm and carry on). We really tried to do as the marines said they did in a hard time *just suck it up*. Dave heard that many times when he was a navy chaplain serving with the marines.

The mission also had a bookstore in Fes. It was just up a hill and across the street from the church. It supplied books for the University, as well as various reading material that might appeal to tourists. The manager of the bookstore was a nice Christian Moroccan man. (He had been terribly beaten and punished because of his beliefs several times.) The missionary who was the "owner" (not literally) of the bookstore was due for furlough, so he and his family left for the States. The duty fell to Dave to fill, while the family was gone for four months. Upon going through medical exams, it was determined this man had a bad case of hepatitis and wouldn't be able to return to the field. So, Dave wound up being pastor, mission treasurer, bookstore owner, Arabic student, and missionary.

Dave's other job as Bookstore owner

In 1993, we went on furlough, mainly to go to our youngest daughter's wedding and so her father could perform the ceremony. The area director for Morocco said that since we didn't get to go to either one of Dave's families' funerals, we could go earlier than scheduled. Our younger daughter married in Virginia Beach, then we went to North Carolina and stayed with our other daughter and her family. In Missouri we visited my parents, brother, and Dave's family. While visiting my mother at the retirement center where she stayed, we rented a room there for a few nights. The pickup truck we borrowed from our daughter was broken into, and Dave's suitcase stolen, along with our cameras and other things. So, all of Dave's clothes and shoes had to be replaced.

After visiting the family, we then headed to Virginia and North Carolina to be with our daughters and their families for a few weeks. Before leaving on furlough, we left the English classes and preaching services in the hands of another Baptist missionary couple. Upon returning, we found they had not done either one but left it amiss.

After our return trip to Morocco, heading back to our apartment in a taxi, we noticed a Mercedes car, several motor scooters, and a donkey pulling a cart besides other cars at a stop light. I thought, *This is where the Lord sent us, to work with this mixture of people.*

When the sing-song call to prayer came from the minarets five times a day, men on the street shook out a small prayer rug and knelt toward the east facing Mecca. After bowing with their foreheads on the ground, they recited a memorized prayer. How my heart ached for them, to know the true God who could be their friend and Savior.

Dave continued to get the books in the bookstore computerized, so the bookstore manager knew how many to order, and it was easier to see the record. He bought an $800 scanner in the States, but it was stolen in the burglary when he lost his clothing. (Because the pickup was not ours but our daughters', we couldn't be reimbursed from the insurance company.) So, he bought another scanner before departing the States so that the bookstore could use it. It took hours and hours to get the books computerized.

Aziz came by periodically to ask for prayer for a sick member of his family or for a difficult test he was taking at the University. One day, nearing graduation, he asked for prayer for a job he was applying for in another city. It was with the water department, and he was successful in securing it. We were so proud of him and all the new believers.

You see, Moroccans are taught to recite prayers from the Koran, and our students found it unusual that a person could pray specifically for a certain thing, for a sick one, or for another person. This we did in our English class, and as Dave did as he counseled someone.

We missed many things about "being home." Mostly, it was with being with our family members, and we missed hearing about world events too. We did listen to BBC news, so that was good and got a kick out of their pronunciation of aluminum and schedule. They just seemed to put extra vowels in it. The only television shows that were aired were all in Arabic of course. It was funny to watch Green Acres dubbed in Arabic.

Moroccans probably thought all Americans were like them!

When there were nine new believers, we asked them if they would like to come to our home and have a worship service. They agreed, and we met at two o'clock on Sunday afternoon to sing choruses and have a Bible study and prayer. We used French, Arabic, or English Bibles and let them read the scriptures. I was able to use flannelgraph pictures on a backboard just as when I was teaching Sunday School to children in the States. They were amazed, just as the children were, as the figures were placed on the board as the story was read by one of the students. The new believer's favorite song was "Lord, I Want to be a Christian in my Heart."

During the summer, several retired American missionaries from the Middle East, seminary professors who spoke Arabic, came to teach Bible Camp to new and older Moroccan believers, from cities all over Morocco. Four men who were believers attended this camp where they memorized Bible verses and had in-depth discussions about leading a Christian life. Six young women attended at a different time. Four were believers; two were seekers, but they made a commitment to the Lord before leaving camp.

I realized that maybe I didn't know English as well as I thought when a pint-sized little English girl corrected my speech. This three-year old came to our apartment to stay awhile, while her parents searched for an apartment. They had visited our church service and said they were going to look for a place to rent the next day. I offered to watch their daughter while they were gone, so that's how I became temporary Grandma for a day. We played games, and then I asked her if she would like to help me make cookies. She agreed, and we mixed up the dough and placed them on the cookie sheet. When they were baked, I took them out of the oven and when cooled offered her a cookie. She promptly said, "These are not cookies, but cakes you know." It seems they call crackers *cookies*. Dave and I had a laugh over it.

Her parents did find an apartment they liked, so they proceeded to try to find furniture, cabinets, and all the things needed to make a house a home. They were missionaries from England, and like everyone else, came to Fes to study Arabic. It was just a few months later that they had to return to England to raise more funds so they could stay in Morocco. To our knowledge, they never were able to return to the country.

A French student asked if they could take English classes too, and I agreed telling him to have the students come on a certain day. Ten students arrived, and I could tell immediately that some of them knew English very well, and the others not at all. So, I split this group into beginners, intermediate, and advanced classes. We all agreed on times they could meet according to their schedules. They were from five different countries in Africa, and it was interesting to find out how and why they came to Fes. One young man's father was an Imam (religious leader) in Cameroon. He spoke English pretty well, so he was in the advanced class. It made me feel good, having an opportunity to teach these men and women from other parts of Africa, but Dave and I felt it would be good to have a single person or couple to work specifically with the students. When they had a party in their French service, each one dressed in their native dress or outfit, and it was exciting to see them in their colorful outfits.

We, Southern Baptist workers, were fortunate not to have to worry about raising funds while we were on furlough, like so many of the other missionaries. The Cooperative Program and the Lottie Moon offering took the worry out of that task and came up with the funds to support us. How thankful we were for the faithful men and women who gave to these funds.

We were given the right, by the mission, to get a new car and gave up the one everyone in the mission called, "the bomb." It was a joy to have a new Fiat to drive to the mission meetings in which every town was held. This was all because of the Lottie Moon offering Southern Baptists lovingly gave at Christmas time. How thankful we were.

We were privileged to have a group of Southern Baptist tourists visit our country. There were twenty-two men and women; our Associate Director and several others from the board who went to all the cities where Southern Baptists were serving. They were on a prayer walk all around Morocco, and we were so glad to have them come. They were shown the church, bookstore, and all the *hot spots* of Fez. They stayed in a hotel near the church, and Abdul and I led them on a tour of the old city as well as having them go to Abdul's home. They got to see what one is like, and they were given cookies and mint tea, as every visitor is given. Then they went to our apartment and had chicken, vegetables and couscous prepared by the women in my English class. It was a joy to have them, and they got to see new Moroccan believers too. Before they left, we all prayed together.

In 1995, I attended a MENA (North Africa and Middle East) conference in Larnaca, Cyprus, as a representative of our mission. It was a joy to see so many workers get together for a nuts and bolts meeting. We learned at that meeting that some changes had been made at the mission board. It upset everyone so much one of the male missionaries from Egypt said, "Maybe we should quit the mission board and join WMU! (Women's Missionary Union). They are the only ones who really care about missions!" I sat next to a man who I later realized had a virus, and as a result, I caught the virus too, leaving me with a flu bug that never went away! When I got back to Fes, I went to a Moroccan pulmonologist who had a German wife who worked and translated for him. He determined that I had asthma. So, he prescribed inhalers for the condition, which I bought at a local pharmacy.

We had a real scare that next summer when the king invited all couples who wanted to get married to join his daughter's wedding party in a ceremony in Fes. Terrorists from Algeria planned to jeopardize the wedding with bombs and kill a large number of Moroccans. But the police got wind of it and captured them. A large amount of bombs, hand grenades, etc. were found and seized.

That summer was difficult for my health. When the temperature rose to 117–118 degrees, it was very hard to breathe. Two American and one Moroccan doctor told me that if I didn't leave Morocco, it would kill me. So, we called the mission board and they said, "Don't quit." They would help us find a place where we could serve the Lord, that was cooler.

We did make a trip home to the States for medical reasons and to see about transferring to another country.

Because Dave had an MBA, we all thought it best if we would consider Western Republic Mission as the next assignment where Dave could be the business manager and treasurer for the countries of Belarus, Moldova, and Ukraine.

Ukraine was under Communist regime from 1917 to 1991 and was open to religious organizations coming into the country after 1991. Some of the first religious groups that entered were the Mormons and the Seventh Day Adventists. They had a right to do that; they just beat us Baptists to it!

We prayed mightily about transferring to Ukraine, hating to leave our Moroccan friends and the work with new believers, but seeking the Lord's guidance. It was a hard decision to make because we really loved those friends and believers after serving there for five years.

(Moroccan names have been changed to protect identity.)

We decided to go to this new assignment and arrived there with just our suitcases. Our other belongings would be flown to Ukraine later on. We stayed in a furnished apartment and started Russian class right away. I wondered why we didn't study the Ukrainian language, but you can't buck the system upon first arriving at a new assignment. The apartment where we stayed was filled with items that gathered dust, such as carpets on the walls that had not been cleaned for a long time. And the area of the apartment building was in disarray. So, my asthma condition worsened. After a few days, we sent word to the associate director that we needed to find another apartment, and it was agreed upon that we needed one.

It was time for the Ukrainian mission to have a mission meeting, and they had been going to Poland for it. So, we traveled by railroad to a little town in this neighboring country.

As we pulled out of the station, I noticed the Communist hammer and cycle sign on each end of the railroad station, and it sent a chill run down my spine. We visited with other missionary families on the train, getting acquainted with the children and their parents. When we arrived at our destination, we all stayed in a large hotel just outside the city. It was good to get to meet the couples and their children at the meeting and at mealtimes. Most of them served in cities far from Kiev, where we were, and also in Moldova and Belarus. We met the director and associate director for the area who lived in Wiesbaden, Germany, and their wives and heard of the plans for the future. After the meetings each day, we visited the closest town. My thoughts kept running back to when the Germans attacked this lovely town and many others in Poland, herding the people into trains to take them to concentration camps. What an atrocity that was! We were in Poland for the mission meeting three or four days, and then headed back to our respective countries by train. As we zipped along the tracks, we noticed the beautiful pastoral view from the window of green fields over valley and hills and farmers cutting and making mounds of hay.

Upon returning to Kiev, we left the furnished apartment and moved into a two-bedroom apartment, again with just our suitcases. The apartment was in the army housing area where it had been opened up to anyone wanting to buy one. The mission paid $50, 000 for it, which was a normal price for most apartments.

Much to our amazement the banks did not have checking accounts or ATMs, and none of the stores that we saw accepted credit cards. We did not have much cash on hand and weren't told to bring around $5,000 cash with us. So, we were in a "hum" (as Dave says).

We did have two air mattresses in our suitcases and used those for sleeping. One of the air mattresses had a leak in it, so every night around two or three o'clock, Dave would awaken me to help him get the air mattress blown up again. In the morning, he tried to find the leak so he could patch it but to no avail. This went on for several days.

We traveled to Russian class by subway, which was not healthy for people with breathing conditions. It was quick but built way down in the ground with strong diesel fumes all around. Most people use the subway as their mode of transportation. Dave and I were the only students in a room of a vacant church building. It was wintertime and mighty cold, and the teacher didn't know much English. But we did have books and our tutor, back at the apartment, could help us learn Russian. There are also buses and trolleys to get around the city of Kiev, where we were.

Dave and Gwyn in front of apartment building

Map of Eastern Europe

After a few days of sleeping on the floor, we happened to see a Visa sign in a window of a mattress and bed shop, while waiting on a streetcar. Hallelujah was our cry as we shopped for a queen-sized bed. There was no delivery service, so the next step was for Dave to go out in the street and find a truck to take it to our apartment! The only one he could find was a huge tenton truck, where the bed had to be tied onto it. Making the truck driver understand English was another problem. It did look ridiculous to see that big, long truck bed with a bed in the middle of it, but sometimes you have to do weird things to get by! I rode in the front of the truck cab, trying to explain where we lived while Dave was on the back of the truck holding it so it wouldn't fall off, even though the bed was tied on. After it was brought inside, we rejoiced over having a bed to sleep in that night and all the other ones.

We finally got our shipment of household goods and were happy to see them again.

Payday finally came so we could buy groceries, and Dave could pay all the missionaries' salaries in the three countries. We found a divan that opened and made into a double bed, two overstuffed chairs, and ottomans on the back of a trailer in the marketplace. We couldn't sit on any of them since they were up high on the trailer but bought them anyway. Other missy's (missionaries) could stay overnight with us now when they came to town. We found a large square table, refrigerator, and washing machine too. There weren't electric outlets or room for a dryer, so I hung the wet clothes on the clotheslines in the balcony. It had glass windows that opened so it was nice in fair weather. The thick socks and Dave's jeans were placed on the radiators in each room. They didn't get hot enough to burn them.

We were fortunate to have plenty of warm heat and water in the apartment. No one was charged for either of those. The heating system was an old communist community set up. One central heating system was in the middle of some apartment buildings and piped into the buildings. There was no way to regulate the radiators, so when they got too hot. We'd open the windows even if it was below zero! We noticed our neighbors did it too.

The water system was a different story. We had water when it was prudent for us to have it. All of the missionaries used water filters, which were supplied by the board. The water came from the Dnieper River, which ran by Chernobyl up north of Kiev. Sometimes I'd be cooking supper and the water stopped flowing. So, I learned to always have a teakettle full on the back of the stove. But sometimes the water was lacking for several days, which made it difficult. Then I learned to save more water in every pan and jug I had so we would have some for cooking and taking what I called a "bird bath." (A little heated water poured in the bottom of the bathtub and flipped upon oneself to get clean.)

We had free phone service to Moldova and Belarus as well as the rest of Ukraine. This was good for Dave's job since he had to call other missionaries in the region. But it was not free to call the United States, of course.

Dave flew to Wiesbaden, Germany, to be with the regional treasurer for a few days and learn the system they advised soon after the mission meeting in Poland. That was a hard introduction into Ukraine for me. We had an ice storm while he was gone, and I had quite a time getting to a store nearby for a few groceries. The steps to the apartment building, railing, street, and sidewalks were all covered with a thick coat of ice. What an experience that was, trying to walk and get to the store and then back to the apartment. It makes a person realize that times like that increase your prayer life. When it snowed, the snow was light and fluffy and dry. I tried to make a snowball, but the snow wouldn't stick together.

After a few months, we were given the use of a mission car and there again it was called the mission "bomb." It didn't have any heat, but it was good to have a car to go to the market and the import stores. There was a huge garage behind the apartment, and Dave found out it was free too. He asked one of the attendants of the garage how many inches of snow they had each snowfall, and one of them said, "Oh, we don't measure it in inches but in meters."

We found our way to the import store after one of the missionaries informed us of it being there. We were glad to find it, even though it was expensive. We could buy name-brand spaghetti sauce, frozen foods, etc. It was sort of like a 7-Eleven store here in the States.

I was anxious to find some fabric so I could make some drapes for the living room and two bedrooms. I sure wanted to find a thick fabric for our bedroom so it would block the early sunshine (at 3 a.m.) from streaming through the window. Kiev, Ukraine, is the same latitude as Newfoundland, and at night, a person can see the aurora borealis lights making the dark sky as light as day. We finally got the apartment looking good after I made all the drapes, and we bought cabinets for books, dishes, and clothes.

Dave was constantly on the computer and going through little slips of paper trying to determine where the mission money had been spent over the last three years. The mission was only three years old and had never had a treasurer. It took him a long time to get the finances all in order.

After getting the drapes made one morning as I pulled them back in the living room, I glanced at all the apartment buildings in the area, and the Holy Spirit spoke to me again. "When are you going to start teaching English to all these people and spreading the word?" There were at least fifteen apartment buildings in the area, so I suppose I'd better get started! Since the buildings were the Ukrainian Army housing area, I wondered if they might send me to Siberia for teaching from the Bible. So, after much prayer, I asked my tutor, Oxsana, to help me write invitation notices to put on the bulletin boards beside all the entrances to the buildings.

She was a university student who lived down the hall. She wondered why we came to Ukraine and asked me that question. I told her my husband was going to help the pastors of the churches (which he was by preaching with a translator). She responded by saying, "Everyone here wants to go to America, and you want to come here!" When I asked about names for girls in Ukraine, she explained that officially your father's name was used, putting an ova at the ending. So, my name would be Calvinova, while Dave's name would be the same, David, but pronounced "Day-ood." She also mentioned that many men had feminine names in not only in Ukraine but all over Europe.

It was only a few days before the response to the notice of English classes began. I was fearful, but confident that the Lord would protect us in this endeavor because of the verse in Psalm 55: 22, "Cast your cares before the Lord and He will sustain you, He will never let the righteous fail." The first one that came to the door was a young woman who said, "I believe in that," as she pointed to a small wooden cross on our foyer wall. She and her husband wanted to come to class and had to work the timing of it around their schedules at the university. They were both medical students, and both of them spoke fairly good English, so I placed them in the advanced class. As others responded it was not difficult to place them in a certain class according to how easily or with difficulty, they spoke English. Nineteen people came to our door wanting to sign up for class. I divided them into three groups according to their ability to speak English and for the reason that we only had six chairs! There was a beginner class (those who didn't know any English), intermediate (those who knew a little), and the advanced group.

When I asked our Russian teacher why it was hard to make a friend in Ukraine, she explained that ever since she was little, she had heard that Americans were their enemies. That was why we had such a hard time getting to know our neighbors. When we smiled or nodded our head at someone we passed, they were tight lipped and would not look at us.

Slowly the students realized we were not in Ukraine to do harm to them but to help them. The students came to class at the designated times—three classes once a week. I had the lessons copied and laid out on the table with pencils at the ready. The beginners started with book one of the Laubach series, intermediate students began with the vowel study and in book two of the Laubach series. The advanced class had a different book, which was Bible based but had homework. Most of the students were in the university and were anxious to learn English. The computer language is written in English, therefore, people want to learn it. Some had taken an English class at the university but wanted to learn more.

Even the beginner class students had university degrees. The university is free, so everyone wants to attend. There were six women in this class, and all were army wives. We all had something in common. Besides being mothers, we were military wives. They studied the first Laubach lesson and then I did something I'd never done before. Pulling things from the kitchen pantry that I did not know the name of in Russian, I put flour, sugar, coffee, etc. on the table and let them tell me what the names were. Then I told them the English name for them. Putting the names of the items on sticky notes, I pressed them on the front of the containers, so I could memorize them and remember them when I shopped.

We found the market, and it was huge. The farmers brought their produce and meat cut into pieces and laid them out on big tables. The meat was bloody, and it was hard to distinguish whether it was pork, beef, or mutton. The only way you could tell the difference is if the farmer had the head of the animal laying with the meat. Usually, the pork and lamb heads were shown, but not the cows. The pork farmer had rolls of fat laid out by his meat. Someone told me that it's a delicacy to serve a big piece of fat and a glass of vodka to a visitor. Thank heaven we were never offered either of the two "delicacies." We did buy pork and a strip of fat to make sausage. When we found the dairy section, I was enthralled to try the whipping cream. It was so thick you didn't have to whip it; just add a little sugar and put it on fruit or dessert.

Dave making sausage

At a Ukrainian Village

With winter coming soon, I thought it prudent that I purchase a long winter coat that I saw displayed outside the market. I found a suitable one— that was reasonably priced. It had a hood with fake fur around the edge and a nice thick insulated lining. Some woman came by and said I should get a longer one.

The weather was comfortable, being the beginning of fall, but it was not long after that we had to pull the sweatshirts and thermal underwear out of the trunks.

It seemed peculiar that one day the many apartment houses were all abuzz with activity but after a snowstorm, they looked like large logs laying under a blanket of snow in the freezing cold.

We discovered that Ukraine did not have the pharmacies that were so prevalent in Morocco. Nor, did they have physicians that you could visit. There was one Christian doctor who would come to your apartment when called, examine you, and give medicine he carried in his bag. This was more than likely medicine that had been donated by some other missionary or a visiting doctor from the States. The only way I could get the inhalers for asthma and other meds I needed was from volunteer medical teams from the States. They came periodically, and we were thankful for their arrival. The same was true for the dental teams that came to give exams and treatment to the Ukrainians and missionaries too. The next year I had a root canal given to me by a dentist from North Carolina, sitting in a backyard lounge chair. What a relief, not to have a painful tooth.

Soon, it was time for the mission chairman, treasurer, their wives, and several others from the mission to go to a planning conference. The meeting was held in Budapest, Hungary. It was an enjoyable trip, and we got a lot done. I thought it was great to see the sights of Europe. The beautiful parliament buildings were on the river just like in London.

The English classes went smoothly with the beginner's class finishing the first book of the Laubach lessons. We had a party for the students, with diplomas given out to the six students, and refreshments given. (The diplomas were left over from using them in Morocco and were originally what we gave to children at Vacation Bible School programs, but the English class students thought they were really great.) One of the students dropped her notebook and papers and let out an expletive you'd hear on many streets in the States. When I asked where she had heard that she said, "On Dallas." That's right, it was shown on television along with Green Acres, dubbed in Russian.

The advanced class took longer to get through their material, since many had to be absent due to classes or taking exams. One day, the medical student Valerie and his wife asked me to lay down on the sofa, face down so he could examine my back. He noticed the pain I was having during class. He asked if it was painful, and I told him only when I walked, sat down, or laid down. Anyone having back pain knows how it feels! He pushed on several places on the spine and determined that I must have a slipped disk! So, he called his father, who was a Ukrainian general and who had a bad back too. The student asked if he could get an appointment with the orthopedic doctor for a friend. I didn't know what to think but went along with the idea because of the severe pain. The student, Valerie, asked Dave if he would drive us to the army base, and he agreed. Upon driving up to the tall iron fence, Valerie asked Dave to stay in the car, while his wife, Olga, and I got in the general's car. The general drove through the gate and getting out we went into the nearest building. She told me not to say anything in English. (That wouldn't be hard, since I didn't know much in the Russian language, except "how much are those potatoes?") She introduced me, giving me a Ukrainian name, and the doctor led me into a small room with a low twin bed by one wall. He motioned for me to lie down on my stomach and felt the backbone. Soon, using the back of his elbow, he smacked the sore spot hard. Then he asked me to go to another room, lie down on my stomach, and he placed a warm pad on my back. It felt wonderful, but I kept thinking, *Would I ever see Dave again?* Going through that tall iron fence was scary! I was sure if I muttered an English word, the game would be up and I'd be on my way to Siberia!

I was so happy not to have that back pain; I asked Valerie what I could do to thank his father and the doctor. He replied, "Just give them a quart of vodka!" Sure, I thought, that would be the end of our work here. So, I bought three huge boxes of chocolates and gave them to each of them.

We attended the International Baptist Church, which was English speaking. They asked Dave to preach several times. Another woman and I taught Sunday School, trading off Sundays so we could attend worship service every other week. That was the most difficult thing I'd ever done on the mission field. We had no literature, and the six children spoke Ukrainian, while I was learning Russian. There are some differences in the languages. I used pictures, drew pictures, and we used sign language to get through the lesson. Their ages were three through twelve. Thank heavens the oldest knew a little English. How I yearned for some good Sunday school teacher's book that I'd used for years.

Kiev, Ukraine
Dave preaching

Russian Orthodox Church

Dave was asked to preach in a Ukrainian church with a translator too. It was good to go to the countryside and meet the church members. We were told by other missionaries not to wear makeup, earrings, or engagement rings to church and always wear a headscarf. Well, at least, you didn't have to fix your hair on Saturday night, as I'd done for years. This practice was to blend in with the dress of the other women.

We had not been in country long when we found out a great deal of money had been donated to Western Republics mission for the use of money to be used by missionaries for a vacation.

What a wonderful thing to do, and all of us appreciated it. In another few months we were scheduled to have an executive meeting in Paris, so we thought we'd wait until after the meeting to start our vacation.

When that time approached, we were thrilled to hear of the work going on all over Europe by Southern Baptist missionaries. After the meeting, we toured Paris, and it was great to see and be on the Eiffel Tower, the Notre-Dame Cathedral and mostly the many museums. Our favorite was the Louvre.

Then we flew to Italy. Dave had been there many times during his twenty-two years in the Navy, but I had never been there. So, we found a USO office and signed up for a tour of Italy that took in Rome, Florence, Pisa, Capri, and many others. Our favorite was Venice. We spent our forty- second anniversary touring Italy and floating along in a gondola in Venice. How thankful we were that someone had compassion for the workers in our area to donate money for a time to get away.

At the beginning of the Christmas season, we put up a small tree and decorated it as well as a nativity scene. When Oxsana came for a Russian lesson, she looked intently at each piece of the nativity set. She said she'd never seen one and said they had not been allowed to have Christmas decorations or celebrate Christmas while communism controlled their country.

They could celebrate New Year though. So, she and her little brother were looking forward to getting New Year presents.

Some of the MKs (missionary kids) thought it would be good to celebrate the holiday on Christmas, New Year, and January 6th (the Russian Orthodox Christmas) too with presents of course.

With the new year we continued in our work, and it was time for us to host the mission meeting. Each month the meeting was held at one of the missionaries' homes, and I decided to serve yeast-glazed donuts and coffee to everyone. But with the cold weather and colds going around not many came to the meeting. So, we were left with oodles of donuts, and it seemed a good time to share with our neighbors. After this, they were more cordial to us, perhaps because they knew we weren't there to hurt them.

In late spring, we learned it was time for another meeting of the mission of Ukraine, Moldova, and Belarus to meet in Poland again. We again traveled by train to a city in a valley of Poland and met in a large hotel. The meeting lasted several days, and at the conclusion of it, another couple and ourselves decided to take three days' vacation and go to Krakow, where the concentration camps of Auschwitz and Birkenau were located.

It was a mind-blowing experience to take in these places! We saw the barracks with hard wooden berths they slept in, large glass cases of suitcases, another of nothing but glasses, shoes, etc. But the most gruesome was viewing the gas chamber where so many thought they were going to get a shower and realized they were getting gassed to death. At Birkenau were the incinerators, where the bodies were obliterated to ashes! It was an eye-opening experience to realize what was done to these people. What a shame for someone to be so cruel to another human being, and there were so many people put to death. I dreamed of this cruel place and what happened for months.

In the summer months, it was pleasant weather, and the funniest thing we saw from the window of a bus was a man selling flat smoked fish, standing near the exit of a subway. He must have been awfully warm standing in the sun because he was fanning with one of his smoked fish.

There was always a surprise of what you could find people selling, coming up the escalator out of the subway. One day, I found blueberries and cranberries too. I bought all they had, which wasn't many, and froze some of them.

My student friend, Valentina, asked if we liked bananas, and when I told her yes, she asked if Dave could drive us to the wholesale market. Vegetables, fruits, and fish were available from other countries. The fruits came from Israel and Turkey, and they were enormous.

Valentina spoke with a man in Russian, and I couldn't understand her; she talked so fast. But she told him we wanted one-half stalk of bananas. We divided them when we got back to the apartment, and we had several pounds. We fixed those ever which way and quickly grew tired of them.

Then Valentina asked if we liked fish, so we went back again to the wholesale market. You'd think I would have learned my lesson, but no, we wound up with a whole box full of frozen Tilapia fish from Peru. We divided them and had fish poked in the freezer in every crevice.

In the fall, I discovered something was wrong with my right eye; things looked blurry. So, I called the doctor, and after he examined me said there was nothing he could do. He suggested we go to the hospital to see an ophthalmologist. So, he made an appointment, and we met on that day at the hospital. It was large and dark inside, with no one else there. We walked up five flights of stairs, because the elevator didn't work. The other doctor was the only one there, and she took me into a closet and used a flashlight to look into my eye. She kept saying, "Problema, problema." When we met the other doctor outside the closet, she explained in Russian of the problem. The English-speaking doctor explained to me that the ophthalmologist found a hemorrhage behind the retina. The only way to stop it was to insert steroid shots all around the eye for several days. She said it would take several days in the hospital to do this.

I must have had a horrible look on my face because she said, "It will be a little needle."

I wasn't happy about the diagnosis or going in that hospital, so I faxed our mission director in Wiesbaden, Germany. He gave me permission to go to Germany and be treated there. Within several days, I sat on a plane heading to Germany, but the plane was delayed since it needed deicing fluid sprayed over the wings. It was mighty cold outside, and we had to fly a long way over the mountains. After a lot of prayer, the flight began, and we reached our destination.

At the appointed time, I saw the ophthalmologist, and after a thorough exam, he said I did have a hemorrhage behind the right retina. And he could treat it with eyedrops with steroid. So, he gave me the eyedrops and they worked just fine. Thank heavens, that I didn't have to go in that hospital in Ukraine.

Upon returning to Kiev, we each worked our jobs—Dave doing the treasurer's job and preaching occasionally, and I taught English classes during the rest of the winter and spring. Then one morning while eating oatmeal for breakfast, I noticed something hard in my mouth. It was a sliver off the front of my lower tooth in front. I started crying, (thinking I was falling apart) and Dave said, "Maybe it's time we go back home to the States where we can get medical and dental help." There were long periods of time when my asthma attacks flared up, and I couldn't get medical help or medicine. We prayed about it long and hard, since we'd been there less than three years. He was soon to have his sixty-fifth birthday, and I was sixty-one.

When the final decision was made, he called our area director and told him that we were planning on resigning due to the medical and dental restrictions in the country. He understood and wished us well and plans were made to go back home. We told all our friends and students, giving and receiving hugs and best wishes. When I mentioned to one of my students that no one had called or investigated the things we had for sale, she said it's probably because the military hadn't been paid for three months. But we received a letter from a missionary couple coming to Kiev that was interested in buying our furniture. We negotiated that through e- mail, and all our furnishings were sold. The only other thing to do was to call the moving company. We didn't have much to move, and the only trouble with the customs department was getting Dave's guitar and banjo out of the country. He explained to them that he brought them to the country and should be able to take them out too.

Soon, the treasurer's books were turned over and plane tickets were mailed to us. It was a long flight to Paris with an overnight stay, and then the next day we flew to Norfolk, Virginia.

What a happy time to see our family again with lots of hugs and kisses!

After a few days, we started looking for a pickup truck. Dave wanted a Ford with a Cummings diesel engine, but we couldn't find one. Then we searched for a camping trailer that could accommodate us for a few months. We found a thirty-foot pull. Behind that was roomy and could sleep us and two others on a sofa with hide-a-bed. You've heard of getting the cart before the horse?

Well, we did that, buying a trailer before we actually found a truck. But eventually, we found a Dodge with a Cummings diesel engine in North Carolina. Finally, we got the two together and started out on our trip to visit family in Missouri. Remember, we didn't have a house anymore, car, or household furnishings, so we started out like newlyweds, starting from scratch.

We were on our last furlough with the International Mission Board and were having fun visiting our girls and grandchildren and getting acquainted with America again. Traveling to Missouri was fun, camping in our new trailer. When we arrived in the Kansas City area, we found a campground at Smithville Lake. We could fish whenever we wanted between visiting with family members, and we weren't a bother to anyone to put us up. After visiting Mom, Dad, and my brother, and Dave's family whenever we could, we started on a trip we'd planned for some time. We wanted to go to places where we'd lived when we were younger that we really enjoyed.

As we traveled, Dave kept looking in the rear-view mirror, to see if the "monster" was still following us. As we drove and camped through Kansas and Oklahoma, the bread baskets of the United States. then came Texas and New Mexico. In Arizona, we saw the beautiful painted rocks. I imagined a stagecoach would come around one of those big rocks, being chased by several hollering Indians. But it was only the area that brought that image. We had never been to the Grand Canyon, and it was a majestic site to behold. We stayed there several days, taking in all the sights and views.

In California, we traveled to Death Valley and stayed at an AFB near there. It was mighty hot, but we were used to that and had air conditioning in the trailer. After this, we went to Stockton and stayed there several days. Mendocino was my favorite place to live as a child, so we went there and then went to Oregon and Washington— the cherry and apple growers of the United States. Dave wanted to visit and stay in Wenatchee and Yakima, Washington, since he worked and picked apples there with his brother, Tom. We stayed there several days, enjoying the sites and beautiful weather.

In Idaho we saw the old silver mines and the Mormon Tabernacle then scooted on over to Montana. We stayed several days at Great Falls and went to the Lewis and Clark Museum. It was great to see how they struggled to get to the Pacific Ocean. But going to Glacier National

Park was the highlight of the trip. It was fantastic to see the snow-covered mountains and the peaceful lake view in the valley below. Then, while still in Montana, we saw many cattle on green rolling hills in the Big Sky State. Leaving there, we drove through and camped in Colorado in the beautiful Rocky Mountains. We traveled the road that went up and up into the heavens before coming down to the endless cornfields in the Sunflower State. That road across Kansas, stretches out flat as an ironing board until one reaches civilization again in Kansas City. At least, that was where the people were that we wanted to see again our family.

Upon arriving back in our home state, we again camped in Smithville Lake, where we could be close to our family members who lived north of Kansas City. Dave had made arrangements to teach some classes and be chaplain for one semester at his alma mater, William Jewell College in Liberty, Missouri while on our long furlough. So when fall classes started, we moved into a small apartment for married students on campus. (We didn't have to; we could have stayed in the camper and traveled every day to the college, but I was getting "trailer-itis.") Just a few months later, we moved again to a missionary house behind the First Baptist Church in Kearney, Missouri.

While Dave was teaching or counseling at William Jewell, I visited my mother in the retirement home and realized she needed more immediate attention. Her eyesight had gotten worse in the eight years we were absent from her, and she now needed a rolling walker to get around. So, after the first of the year, when Dave's chaplaincy at the college ended, we officially resigned from the IMB. It was a joy to work for them, but we both needed medical attention that we couldn't get overseas.

In the spring, we bought a small ranch house that Mom could easily get around in and started renovating it. It took a long time to get the kitchen and both baths in shape. We went to our retirement ceremony in May and retired with two couples with whom we had worked in Morocco. My mother moved back in with us after we retired, so she was with us five more years, before the Lord called her home. We were glad that we could care for her in the later years of her life.

We then sold our house in North Kansas City and moved to the East Coast to be near our two daughters and five grandchildren.

We were glad we were able to answer God's call and serve where people needed us.

To the best of our abilities, we brought the truth of God's love and forgiveness to those we encountered in Morocco and Ukraine.

For those friends of the Lord, we pray that God will give them protection and peace.

Please remember we are here to be God's tools. To tell Good News to others, so they can be forgiven of their sins and follow His guidance for better life. Then we will all be with Him through eternity.

RECIPES FROM ABROAD

Moroccan Chicken and Cous-cous

1 chicken cut up (or several chicken breasts)

2 chicken bouillon cubes

2 to 3 minced garlic cloves

2 medium sized sliced onions

3 to 4 carrots

3 to 4 potatoes

3 to 4 zucchini or yellow squash or any other vegetable

1 small bunch of parsley (or dried)

2 big slices fresh or frozen pumpkin (it's a squash too and is good)

1 teas. saffron

Cook chicken pieces until almost tender with bouillon, salt and pepper, garlic and onions. Add carrots, potatoes, parsley, and any other vegetables you wish. Add pumpkin at last, since it cooks quickly.

Couscous

Fix according to package direction

Raisin topping

Cook 1/2 cup raisins, mixing in a mixture of 1/2 tablespoon corn starch, small amount of water, 2 tablespoon sugar, and several shakes of cinnamon.

When the chicken and vegetables are done, put couscous on a large platter with sides or a large pie plate so broth won't spill. Then top with chicken, broth, and vegetables, making a mound. Then top with raisin sauce making the sauce dribble down the sides. Now, it should look like a volcano erupting, so dig in!

Ukrainian Borsch

1/2 lb. meat (chicken, beef or pork)

1/2 head cabbage (shredded)

1 medium large beet, grated

1 1/2 c. tomato sauce

2 or 3 carrots, grated

2 or 3 potatoes, cut up

1 large onion, diced

Boil meat till nearly tender. Add potatoes and onion, adding beets and grated carrots after broth is ready. Add tomato sauce and spices last (salt, pepper, dill, parsley). This is where Ukrainian Borsch varies from house to house.

ABOUT THE AUTHORS

Name: David Garth Page

Born: October 15, 1933

Education: Southern Baptist Seminary, William Jewell College, South Theological Seminary, Old Dominion University

Residence: North Carolina

Family: Wife, Gwyn; son, Carey (deceased); daughters; Becky and Laura; five grandchildren, two great grandchildren

Hobbies: Bird hunting, fishing

David Page was pastor of several churches during college and seminary and several more years before entering the Navy chaplaincy. Then the Lord led him and his wife to the mission field in Morocco. There, he was pastor of an English-speaking church along with several other duties. When they transferred to another country, he was treasurer and business manager for the countries of Ukraine, Moldova, and Belarus.

Name: Gwyndolin Cloud Page

Born: February 4, 1938

Education: William Jewell College, Baptist College of Charleston, Old Dominion University

Family: Husband, David; son, Carey (deceased); daughters, Becky & Laura; five grandchildren, two great grandchildren

Hobbies: Oil & acrylic painting, reading, writing

The day Gwyn Page married was when she became a preacher's wife. Later she became a mother and a chaplain's wife. After her husband retired from the Navy, they were led to the mission field where she caught a virus that left her with asthma and heart trouble. They were forced to transfer to the cooler climate of Ukraine. She taught ESL in both countries using Laubach reading and Book of Mark series.

www.ingramcontent.com/pod-product-compliance
Lightning Source LLC
Chambersburg PA
CBHW051234120626
46547CB00013B/1643